Candles, Cakes, and Donkey Tails

Candles, Cakes, and Donkey Tails

Birthday Symbols and Celebrations

by LILA PERL

Illustrations by Victoria de Larrea

CLARION BOOKS

TICKNOR & FIELDS: A HOUGHTON MIFFLIN COMPANY

NEW YORK

Clarion Books
Ticknor & Fields, a Houghton Mifflin Company
Text copyright © 1984 by Lila Perl
Illustrations copyright © 1984 by Victoria de Larrea

Library of Congress Cataloging in Publication Data
Perl, Lila.
Candles, cakes, and donkey tails.
Includes index.
Summary: Discusses the significance of birthday symbols
and customs, such as candles, cakes, and spanks, and
includes information on birthday horoscopes, birthstones,
and celebrations in other countries.
1. Birthdays — Juvenile literature. [1. Birthdays]
I. de Larrea, Victoria, ill. II. Title.
GT2430.P47 1984 394.2 84-5803
RNF ISBN 0-89919-250-5
PAP ISBN 0-89919-315-3

P 10 9 8 7 6 5 4 3

This book is for
Andrew Scott Hocking,
born
Thursday, March 11, 1982.

May all your days be happy!

Contents

1   How Birthdays Began   ·   *1*

2   When Were You Born?   ·   *7*

3   What's in a Name?   ·   *21*

4   Why We Light Birthday Candles   ·   *37*

5   Which Birthdays Are Special?   ·   *51*

Index   ·   *69*

1

How Birthdays Began

Have you ever thought back to long, long ago when people lived in caves or other natural shelters, hunting animals and gathering wild plants for their food? Have you ever wondered how, or even if, prehistoric people celebrated their birthdays?

The answer is that they almost certainly didn't. In those days, before recorded history, nobody had yet found a way to measure time. Weeks, months, and years, as we know them, did not exist. There was no such thing as a calendar. So how could birthdays be remembered?

Sometimes, however, an older member of a family or tribe could recall when a child had been born. Perhaps the birth had taken place at the time of a great flood. That had been an important event. The river had overrun its banks and swallowed up the land as never before within living memory.

Or a child might have been born just after the eruption of a rumbling volcano. No one among those who had dwelt near the volcano could forget how the gushing steam and lava had sent everyone fleeing under a rain of fiery ash.

But even if someone had been born at a memorable time, there was still no calendar on which to mark the day. And there was no way to measure the years that followed. So for hundreds of thousands of years of human history, birthday anniversaries went unmarked. And so did many other important events in a person's lifetime.

At last, though, some people began to figure out calendars. They did this by watching the movement of the sun, the phases of the moon, and the changing of the seasons. The Egyptians of six thousand years ago made up a calendar, as did people of other ancient civilizations. One of the very first birthday parties ever written about was given by an Egyptian pharaoh, or king. The Bible, in the Book of Genesis, tells us how he made a great feast for all his servants.

After a time, with the help of calendars, other rulers began to celebrate their birthdays. The ancient Romans even made up birth dates for their gods. They marked them each year with parades and chariot races.

The Roman calendar, however, was not very accurate. Often the number of months and the seasons of the year did not come out even. Finally, Julius Caesar, the famous Roman general and statesman, decided to have the calendar corrected. It was then named after him and called the Julian calendar.

Julius Caesar also gave his name to one of the months. On the old calendar it had been called Quintilis. Now it became known as July. The calendar most of the world follows today is very similar to Julius Caesar's calendar. It is called the Gregorian calendar.

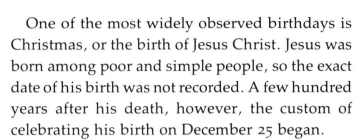

One of the most widely observed birthdays is Christmas, or the birth of Jesus Christ. Jesus was born among poor and simple people, so the exact date of his birth was not recorded. A few hundred years after his death, however, the custom of celebrating his birth on December 25 began.

Some other religions, besides Christianity, celebrate the dates on which their founders are known or believed to have been born. Moslems, followers of the religion known as Islam, celebrate the birthday of the Prophet Mohammed. He is thought to have been born in the year 570.

As the use of a more accurate calendar became more widespread, the birthdays of other well-known figures came to be regularly observed. Among them were saints, nobles, generals, and national heroes. But it is only in quite recent times that ordinary people have begun to celebrate their birthdays.

Even today, in many parts of the world, birth dates go unnoticed. Instead, people may have group birthdays. Each person will simply become one year older on a given date, such as the Chinese New Year. Or, in some branches of the Christian religion, a person may be named after a particular saint. So sometimes the saint's day rather than the day of birth will be the occasion for giving a party and receiving presents.

More and more, though, people the world over attach a certain magic to their actual date of birth. Many think the exact hour is important, too.

They believe that this tells them something special about the kind of person they will be and the kind of life they will have.

Whatever you believe about the time of your birth, one thing is certain. Your birthday is different from every other holiday throughout the year. Even if other people you know were born on the same day, it is still the one day that belongs in a particular way to you. It is personal. It is your very own.

2

When Were You Born?

Is it possible for anybody to *remember* being born? Probably not. We have to depend on other people for information about the time and place.

Very careful birth records must, of course, be kept. They will be important for when we enter school, vote, marry, and at many other points in our lives. But there is also something mystical that seems to fascinate us about our moment of entry into this world.

Perhaps this is because we have all read stories about the good fairies or evil witches present at the births of princesses. We've read old-time legends about heroic fighters who were born amid thunder claps and lightning bolts that struck the earth like flaming lances. These stories and legends show us that people have long believed that one's future can be told at birth.

Can we believe in such birth predictions and prophecies? Or are they really quite silly? Our good sense tells us that our futures are shaped and changed by many factors — our families, our friends, the schools we go to, the world we live in. What have evil fairies or thunderstorms at birth got to do with the way our lives turn out?

Yet most of us cannot resist reading our horoscope in the daily newspaper. We may wear a ring with our birthstone in it for good luck. And when we blow out the candles on our birthday cake, we are careful to keep what we wished a secret. If we tell, of course, our wish won't come true.

In other words, we follow many of the old birthday beliefs. We pay attention to the meanings of the old-time birth symbols. And we carry on the old celebrations. We don't necessarily take them seriously. We do these things mainly for fun. But it is also possible that there is something deep inside us that *wants* to believe.

. . .

Almost everyone knows the familiar day-by-day birthday rhyme that is supposed to tell you your fortune. All you have to do is find out what day of the week you were born on. If you're not sure, look in an encyclopedia. Most have a chart called a perpetual calendar that will help you figure out the day from the date of birth.

The rhyme is so old that nobody knows who wrote it or when. It goes like this:

> *Monday's child is fair of face,*
> *Tuesday's child is full of grace,*
> *Wednesday's child is full of woe,*
> *Thursday's child has far to go,*
> *Friday's child is loving and giving,*
> *Saturday's child works hard for a living,*
> *But the child that is born on the Sabbath day*
> *Is bonny and blithe, and good and gay.*

As with many of the old rhymes and legends, certain parts were changed as they were handed down through the years. So there are often a few different versions. Possibly some people who were born on a Thursday didn't care for their birth prediction. So they changed it. In another version of the rhyme, the lines read:

> *Wednesday's child is dour and sad,*
> *Thursday's child is merry and glad,*

Perhaps even now somebody is working on a better prediction for Wednesday's and Saturday's children.

There is also some question about the especially lucky child who is "born on the Sabbath day." Among almost all Christians, Sunday is the Sabbath, or holiest day of the week. But among Jews, and some Christians – the Seventh-Day Adventists, for example – Saturday is the Sabbath. Among Moslems, Friday is the holiest day. So here is something else to think about when we are trying to figure out our birth prediction. As a Sabbath birth is supposed to bring such good fortune, why not include all the Sabbaths among the luckiest days to be born?

. . .

What about birthstones and birth flowers? Each month of the year has been given its special gem and flower. For example, if you were born in May, your lucky stone is the emerald. Your lucky flower is the lily-of-the-valley.

The idea of lucky stones seems to go all the way back to ancient times. The Bible tells us that each of the twelve tribes of Israel had its own precious stone as its symbol. All twelve jewels were set in fittings of gold and worked into a rich breastplate that was worn by the high priest.

Later, during the Middle Ages, many people dabbled in magic. They believed that certain gems had special properties that could ward off evil spirits. Also, each stone was supposed to bring a special kind of good fortune. Soon people began wearing brooches, pendants, and rings

with the stone that was said to be the symbol of their month of birth.

As time went on, jewelers did so well selling birthstone jewelry for people's birthdays that florists must have decided there should be lucky flowers, one for each birth month of the year. Often there are two or more different stones and flowers for each month. Birth flowers may differ also depending on the region where you live. Here is a chart that lists the most common birthstones and flowers:

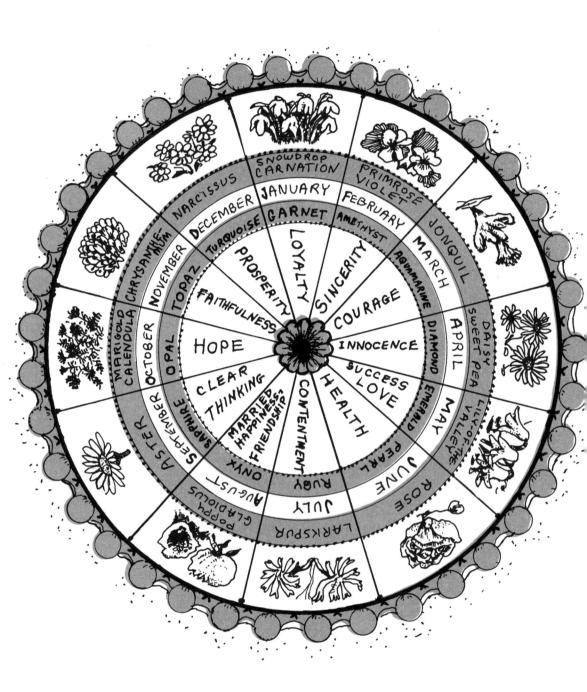

Even if you don't really believe that a particular gemstone or flower bouquet can bring you luck, it still might be nice to receive one as a birthday gift. So jewelers and florists make sure to display the lists of stones and flowers for each month where everyone can see them.

In some parts of the world, tree-planting is connected with the birth of a child. It is believed that as the tree grows and flourishes, so the child will grow and prosper. It is an old custom in certain parts of Switzerland to plant a fruit-bearing tree — an apple tree for a boy, a pear tree for a girl.

. . .

Astrology is another way of trying to foretell the future. The study of the sun, the moon, the stars, and the planets helped the people of ancient civilizations to develop a calendar. Some members of these civilizations believed that the heavenly bodies could also be used to predict coming events. They claimed that by reading the skies they could foresee earthquakes, floods, and other disasters of nature. Sometimes their predictions were correct. Maybe the astrologer-prophets were right just by luck. In any case, many people came to believe in them.

Astrologers also stated that the exact positions of the heavenly bodies at the time of a person's birth were very important. The stars decided your future. They also decided your character, your personality, your talents, your health, and many other things about you. All of this information, and much more, was to be found in your horoscope or birth chart.

Most scientists do not believe it is possible for the heavens to rule the lives of humans in the way that astrologers say they do. Yet often one's personality, and even some of the things that happen in one's life, seem to match the predictions in one's birth sign. Is this just an accident?

According to astrology, the year is made up of twelve birth signs. They are often shown in the form of a circle that resembles a big pie divided into twelve parts. The circle is called a zodiac. Each birth sign has a name and also a symbol such as a goat, a crab, a lion, a pair of twins, even a set of scales. The zodiac year begins on March 21 instead of January 1.

Here are the signs of the zodiac and a short description of the personality traits for each sign. How well do you think your birth sign describes you?

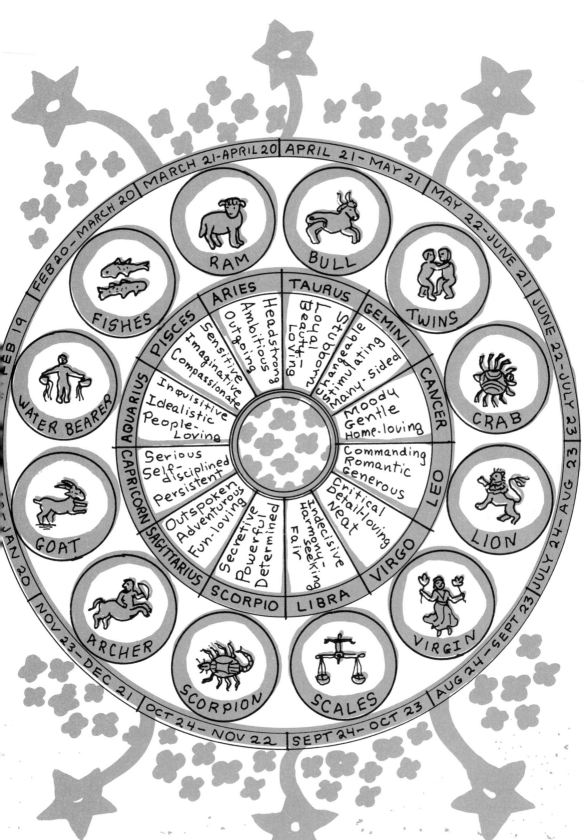

15

Sometimes the dates for the various signs of the zodiac differ a little from those given above. Astrologers tell us this is because the sun enters the signs at slightly different times in different years. So the dates may change by hours or even by a day or so.

Therefore, astrologers say, they must know the year of birth and also the exact hour. These are as important as the month and day if they are to draw up a birth chart that will predict a person's future correctly.

•   •   •

In Chinese astrology, the zodiac is different. From very ancient times, China was sealed off from the rest of the world. So it is not surprising that its people developed their own set of beliefs.

Instead of having a year with twelve different birth signs in it, the Chinese have a zodiac that lasts for twelve years. Each year is named for a different animal. Starting with the year 1985, the rotation of animals is as follows:

Bull (or Ox)	Sheep (or Lamb)
Tiger	Monkey
Rabbit	Rooster (or Cock)
Dragon	Dog
Snake	Pig (or Boar)
Horse	Rat

After each of the twelve animal years has passed, the whole cycle begins again.

Chinese people who follow the old customs

believe that the animal sign of the year in which you were born foretells your character and decides your future. For example, old-fashioned families do not think it is a good idea for a man born in the Year of the Sheep to marry a woman born in the Year of the Tiger. The tiger is a beast of prey. It can kill and devour a sheep. Therefore, the wife might rule or even destroy the husband.

For many centuries, Chinese families arranged marriages according to the years in which the bride and bridegroom had been born. Sometimes a young man would have to marry a much older woman because their animal signs were a good match. Or a very young girl might be forced to marry an old man. Business partners and even friends chose each other according to their birth years. Nowadays many Chinese think these old customs are foolish.

As China's civilization was formed in ancient times, its traditional calendar is very old. China is now in its forty-seventh century! (The Hebrew calendar, even older, is in its fifty-eighth century.) The old Chinese calendar followed the phases of the moon. So the new year did not begin on January 1. It started at the time of the new moon in late January or in February.

Today China follows the same calendar as the Western countries. But its people still celebrate the Chinese New Year in the old way. The same is true for many Chinese people now living in the United States or other parts of the world.

Chinese New Year lasts for several days. It is a time for noisemaking, feasting, wearing new clothes, exchanging presents, and visiting family and friends. Rockets, sizzlers, and other fireworks are set off to drive away the evil spirits of the old year. A large, fierce-looking dragon performs the dragon dance. In China this mythical animal is a sign of good fortune.

Surprisingly, this holiday is more than just a way of welcoming the new year. In China and other parts of the Far East it is also a giant birthday party. In the past, few people except for emperors and other important figures celebrated their dates of birth. The rest of the people in the country simply became one year older on New Year's. Even a baby born near the end of the old year would gain a whole year.

Little by little, especially in countries such as Japan, people of the Far East have begun to celebrate their individual birthdays. In a way, though, the two ideas are the same. Whether we are starting a new calendar year or a new birth year, we are hoping for a year of good health and good fortune. We celebrate bravely and noisily. We are about to step into the unknown and perhaps we are just a little bit afraid.

ABRAHAM · ED ·
VICTOR ·
NICK · CHESTER · IRVING · SALVATOR · J.J. · ORSON ·
NED
VERGIL · LEONARD
CHARLES · CLANCY · ROBERT · FRANK
SANFORD · BOB
JACQUES · PAUL ·
GEORGE ·
CHRIS ·
KEITH ·
LOUIS ·
PHILLIP ·
AMADEUS ·
WOLFGANG
JOE
SEBASTIAN · MICHEL
WILLIE
ZO ·
JOHN ·
HERBERT ·
MATTHEW · DUNCAN ·
PETER ·
MORGAN ·
KRISHNA
KURT · ROBIN ·
BERNARD ·
HAROLD ·
KEITH · DAVID · DONALD · STEVEN · HENRY ·
RICHARD · SAMUEL ·
CLARENCE ·
JUDE ·
BURT
IVAN ·
WINSTON ·
BENJAMIN
IGOR ·
ALBERT
KIRBY ·
CURT ·
GORDON
CHESTER
WALTER · LANFORD ·
ERIC · ERNEST · MARTIN · THOMAS · JAMES · JOSEPH
NED ·
ALAN ·
LAWRENCE ·
IB ·
KENNETH
SHELDON · CORY · EZRA
MARK
WILLIAM ·
KOICHI ·
LEWIS · LEROY
CANIO ·
EDWIN ·
XAVIER · MANUEL ·
HOWARD · ALEXANDER ·

3

What's in a Name?

One of the first things that happens after you're born is that you're given a name. Often your name has been chosen in advance. Probably there were two names waiting for you, depending on whether you turned out to be a boy or a girl. But maybe not. Nowadays doctors are able to perform a simple test before birth to check on the health of the baby. This test also tells the sex of the unborn baby.

Some people think that a child should be given an unusual name. They say that having a name that is different makes you strong. It makes you think of yourself as a special person. You would be more easily remembered because of your name.

But others feel that having an unusual name can cause all sorts of problems. People might keep spelling it wrong or might even make fun of it. You might find yourself having to defend your name. Getting along in school and with friends might be harder because of your name.

Most of us are given the more ordinary names. There seem to be fashions in popular names. Back in the year 1900 the most common names in the United States were John and Mary. Fifty or sixty years later, Robert, Michael, and Mark were very popular boys' names. For girls some of the favorites were Linda, Barbara, and Susan. In recent years, a whole crop of names, some old and some new, have become fashionable. Of today's twenty most popular names – ten for boys and ten for girls – more begin with the letter "J" than any other letter! Jonathan, Jason, Jennifer and Jessica are a few examples of this trend.

Where do names come from and what do they mean? From very early times, people have been given first names. Often the name described the child or told how others felt about him or her. The biblical name David means "beloved." The Old French name Blanche means "white one" or "fair one."

MAY JUNE JULIA APRIL JANET

EDMUND BEN DIRK PERRY OLAF

CLAIRE UNIS ABBIE IRENE RHODA

CELIA MORRIS NORMAN JACK LLOYD

GRETA MARY NANCY PAULA SELMA

If the parents hoped that a boy baby would grow up to be a brave warrior, they might call him William. This name comes from the Old German name Wilhelm. It is a combination of the words for "will" and "helmet." In the names Edward and Howard, the "ward" means "guardian," or defender of the tribe. The Old English name Edward stands for "rich guardian." Howard stands for "chief guardian."

A girl might be named for one of the virtues, or traits of goodness, in the belief that she would live up to her name. Faith, Hope, Charity, Constance, and Patience are some examples. Most of these names come from Latin.

Early peoples thought that giving an infant the name of a courageous animal would help make the child brave and strong. Names like Leo, Leon, Leonard, and Lionel for a boy and Leona for a girl are all from "lion." Wolfe and Wolfgang come, of course, from "wolf." Some animal names are really in foreign languages. So we don't recognize them as being the names of animals, birds, or insects. Deborah is actually the Hebrew word for "bee."

The names of flowers and plants like Rose, Lily, Violet, Fern, Heather, and Holly have been very popular for girls. Flora itself means "flower." Like the animal names, some flower names are

in foreign languages. Daphne is the Greek word for laurel.

Jewels, too, have inspired names for girls, such as Pearl, Opal, and Ruby. Margaret, by the way, comes from the Latin for pearl. And so do all its variations, such as Margie, Marjorie, Margo, Madge, Maggie, and even Meg, Peg, Peggy, and Rita! Less common first names that come from gems are Sapphire, Garnet, and Topaz. The name Gemma, from the Italian, simply means "gem," or "precious stone."

. . .

Nowadays the meaning of the name itself is not as important as in the past. The sound of the name and our feeling about it are what seem to count most. A baby might be named after a president or a movie star. Or a name might come from an admired character in a fairy tale or other story, a play, a movie, or even from a TV program. Often a first name is chosen because its sound goes well with the second, or family, name.

Family customs and religion, of course, have a lot to do with choosing a name for a new baby. In some families, children are named for their parents or other relatives, either living or dead. A boy who is given the same name as his father may be known as Junior or Sonny or Chip (from "chip off the old block") to avoid mixups at home. Sometimes these names stick for life. A silver-haired grandfather may still be "Sonny" to his family and friends, even though *his* father has long since died.

In certain branches of the Jewish religion, children are named in honor of dead relatives only. But this custom is not part of Jewish law, so other groups do name children after living parents and grandparents. Either way, a Hebrew or other foreign name will often be changed slightly. A girl named for a great-grandmother called Mindel might be known as Mindy. A boy named for a grandfather whose name was Reuven might be called Ricky. In that case, only the first letter of

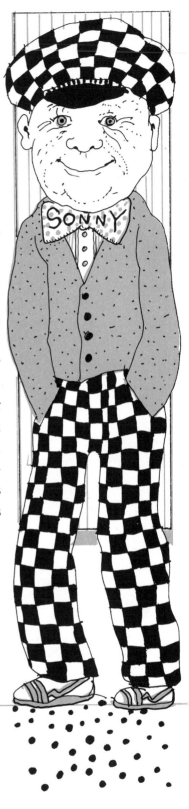

the name would remain the same. But the boy would still be his grandfather's namesake.

Among some Catholic families, as well as certain other Christians in various parts of the world, babies receive the names of saints. Sometimes the saint's day and the child's day of birth are the same. But more often the saint's day or name day, is at a different time from the child's birthday. What happens then? Well, in that case, there may be a birthday-like party on the child's name day rather than on the actual birthday.

Suppose you have been named for Saint Agnes. She is known as your patron saint. Her feast day is January 21. Even though you were born in July, your family might choose to have a celebration on January 21.

On the morning of Saint Agnes's Day, you and your family might go to church and attend Mass Afterward you would return home for a festive lunch or maybe an all-day open house. Friends and relatives would visit, bringing gifts and good

wishes. When your real birthday came along in July, you might or might not have a second celebration.

The custom of naming children after saints began hundreds of years ago. It has long been carried on in Belgium, France, Spain, Italy, Greece, and other countries. The patron saint is believed to protect the child against evil. This idea probably had its beginnings in the folk legends of long ago, in which good fairies or other kindly spirits were called on to watch over the newborn.

Certain countries, too, have patron saints. Many children in those countries are named after them. Saint Patrick of Ireland, Saint George of England, Saint James of Spain, Saint Stephen of Hungary, and Saint Casimir of Poland are especially well known.

Among Spanish-speaking families, children are often named after members of the Holy Family — María (Mary), José (Joseph), and Jesús (Jesus). Regarding the name Jesus, however, many other

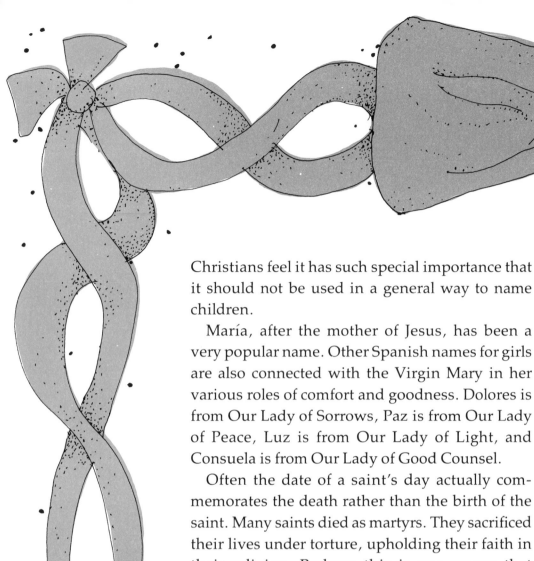

Christians feel it has such special importance that it should not be used in a general way to name children.

María, after the mother of Jesus, has been a very popular name. Other Spanish names for girls are also connected with the Virgin Mary in her various roles of comfort and goodness. Dolores is from Our Lady of Sorrows, Paz is from Our Lady of Peace, Luz is from Our Lady of Light, and Consuela is from Our Lady of Good Counsel.

Often the date of a saint's day actually commemorates the death rather than the birth of the saint. Many saints died as martyrs. They sacrificed their lives under torture, upholding their faith in their religion. Perhaps this is one reason that having an elaborate party with games, music, balloons, party hats, and lots of good things to eat on one's name day doesn't always seem quite fitting.

Little by little, the custom of observing name days with parties seems to be dying out. It is gradually becoming more and more popular everywhere to have the festive celebration on the anniversary of one's birth instead of on one's name day.

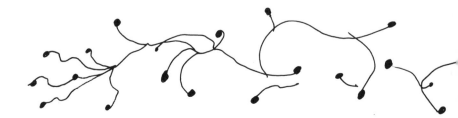

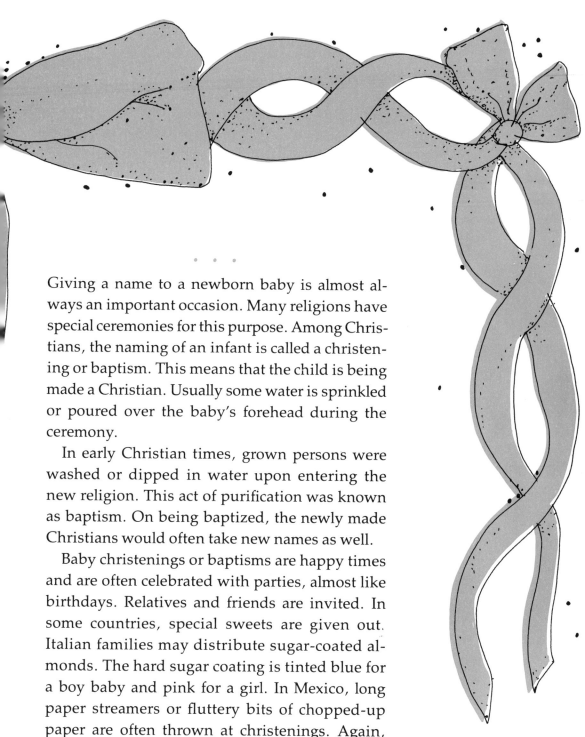

Giving a name to a newborn baby is almost always an important occasion. Many religions have special ceremonies for this purpose. Among Christians, the naming of an infant is called a christening or baptism. This means that the child is being made a Christian. Usually some water is sprinkled or poured over the baby's forehead during the ceremony.

In early Christian times, grown persons were washed or dipped in water upon entering the new religion. This act of purification was known as baptism. On being baptized, the newly made Christians would often take new names as well.

Baby christenings or baptisms are happy times and are often celebrated with parties, almost like birthdays. Relatives and friends are invited. In some countries, special sweets are given out. Italian families may distribute sugar-coated almonds. The hard sugar coating is tinted blue for a boy baby and pink for a girl. In Mexico, long paper streamers or fluttery bits of chopped-up paper are often thrown at christenings. Again, the colors are blue for a boy and pink for a girl.

Among some of the world's peoples, it is be-

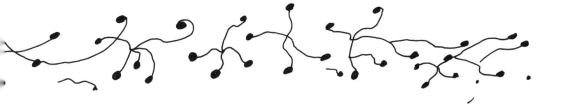

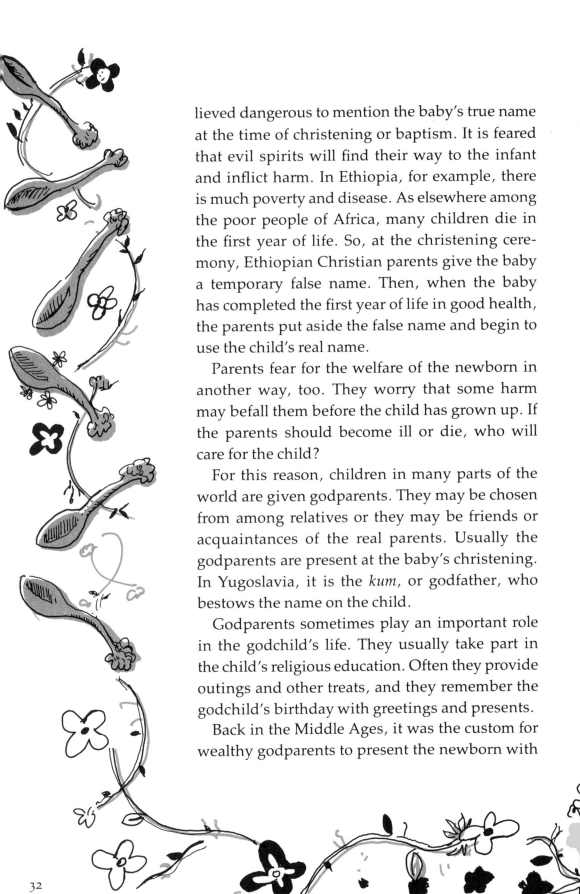

lieved dangerous to mention the baby's true name at the time of christening or baptism. It is feared that evil spirits will find their way to the infant and inflict harm. In Ethiopia, for example, there is much poverty and disease. As elsewhere among the poor people of Africa, many children die in the first year of life. So, at the christening ceremony, Ethiopian Christian parents give the baby a temporary false name. Then, when the baby has completed the first year of life in good health, the parents put aside the false name and begin to use the child's real name.

Parents fear for the welfare of the newborn in another way, too. They worry that some harm may befall them before the child has grown up. If the parents should become ill or die, who will care for the child?

For this reason, children in many parts of the world are given godparents. They may be chosen from among relatives or they may be friends or acquaintances of the real parents. Usually the godparents are present at the baby's christening. In Yugoslavia, it is the *kum*, or godfather, who bestows the name on the child.

Godparents sometimes play an important role in the godchild's life. They usually take part in the child's religious education. Often they provide outings and other treats, and they remember the godchild's birthday with greetings and presents.

Back in the Middle Ages, it was the custom for wealthy godparents to present the newborn with twelve silver spoons at the time of christening. Silver is a precious metal. It is also supposed to bring luck. Nowadays, when we speak of someone who seems to have a fortunate life, we say that that person was ''born with a silver spoon in his (or her) mouth.''

Whatever kind of naming ceremony takes place, the important thing as you grow up is to feel comfortable with your name. Sometimes a name just doesn't seem to fit. It doesn't properly describe your appearance, your personality, or simply the way you feel about yourself.

Problems might also come from having a name that doesn't make it clear whether you are a boy or a girl. It has become more and more popular for girls to receive names that were once given mainly to boys. Leslie, Sydney, Dana, Courtney, Stacey, and Jeremy are some examples. And there have even been cases of girls named Nigel and Errol. Boys who have these names may be embarrassed at being taken for girls. And girls may be equally embarrassed when they are assumed to be boys.

It has been said that if you don't like your name, you may end up not liking yourself. Studies have been made of college students to find out how they felt about their names. More young women than young men said they disliked their first names. But many of the male students were unhappy with their names, too.

Names that are confusing, sound "funny," or just don't feel right can be changed. Sometimes a middle name or even a nickname or pet name can become a new first name that you will like better. If, however, your new name is very different from the one on your birth certificate, it might be best to have it changed legally. Usually this process is not difficult or costly.

You were too young to be consulted about your name when it was given to you. Yet it is an important part of your identity. It is one of those special things about you that help to make you *you*.

4

Why We Light Birthday Candles

Is there such a thing as a birthday cake without candles? Not really. Even a cupcake says "Happy Birthday" when we put a single candle on top and light it.

How did the custom of lighting candles on birthday cakes start, and what does it mean?

Candles were invented thousands of years ago. The first candles were crude torches made of animal fats and plant husks. Later, candles came to be made of wax. Candles not only gave light; they were a source of movable fire. Early peoples believed that the smoke from fires would ascend to the tops of the distant mountains, to the far-away sky. They hoped that the gods who lived in these mysterious places would answer the prayers they had said over the flames.

Children's birthday parties, as we know them

today, really began in Germany a couple of hundred years ago. At these parties, it became the custom to put tiny candles on top of a cake. Usually there was a candle for each year of life and one for the year to come. The birthday child made a secret wish and then blew out the candles. Birthdays, like birth, were seen as a time of danger. So this was another way of trying to ensure good luck on entering a new and unknown year of life.

We are very superstitious about the wishes we make over our birthday candles. The first rule is that as soon as we make our wish, we must blow out all the candles in a single puff. If even one candle remains burning, our wish may not come true. The second rule is that we must never tell our wish.

German candlemakers became famous for all sorts of birthday candles. They not only made very tiny ones to put on cakes. Some of their birthday candles were very tall, thick, and beautifully decorated. A "twelve-year candle" was sometimes given to a child at the time of christening. This candle had a series of markings on it. At each birthday, for twelve years, the candle was placed in a holder and lit. It was burned down to the next marking and then carefully put away for the following year.

Since the first children's birthday parties in Germany, the birthday cake itself has changed quite a bit. Nowadays most party cakes are baked in spongy layers with a filling in between and a decorative frosting on the top and sides. Even a cake made entirely of ice cream may be a birthday cake. In the past, however, many birthday and name-day cakes were made of sweetened bread-like dough sprinkled with sugar crystals. They might contain raisins or other dried fruits cut into bits. Sometimes they were baked in a *Gugelhupf* — a fancy-shaped mold with a swirled or fluted pattern.

It was also the custom to bake tiny objects inside the birthday cake. These objects would tell the fortunes of the host and guests. For example, if you received a slice of cake with a coin in it, it meant you would grow up to be rich. A button, however, meant you would be poor. If you found a ring in your piece of cake, it meant that you would marry. If you found a tiny thimble, you would remain single.

. . .

Probably one reason that we have a party on our birthday is to surround ourselves with well-wishers. For the good wishes of our friends and relatives are supposed to protect us from evil spirits. Some people say that birthday wishes must be offered as early as possible in the day. Birthday cards, of course, are sent out in advance so they will be sure to arrive in time for early greetings. The custom of sending birthday cards began in Great Britain, the United States, and Canada a little over a hundred years ago.

In many parts of the world, it is a tradition to give the birthday child pinches, smacks, spanks, thumps, bumps, or punches. Even though they may hurt a little, they are said to be very lucky. And you must never cry. For the saying goes that if you do, you will "cry all year."

The reason for birthday spanks is to spank away any evil spirits and send them scurrying far into the distance. Punches, thumps, and pinches, the harder the better, are supposed to do the same thing. In Belgium, a family member may tiptoe into the birthday child's room early in the morning. Immediately on awakening, the child will be pricked with a needle for good luck!

The older you are, the more spanks, punches, or bumps you will probably receive. Usually there is one for each year of your life plus "one to grow on," "one to live on," "one to eat on," "one to get married on," and so forth.

In Scotland it is popular to give birthday punches. But in England and Ireland, birthday bumps are most common. They are usually given by schoolmates. Two people hold the birthday child by the arms and two by the ankles. For each bump the child is raised and then lowered to the ground. Sometimes the bumps are pretty hard.

Chair-raising is a more gentle form of bumping, especially for younger children. This is sometimes done at an Israeli birthday party. The small child sits in a chair that is raised and lowered by a father, uncle, or other grown-up. The chair is raised once for each year of life and once more for good luck.

Party snappers, horns, bursting balloons, firecrackers, and other noisemakers are just one more way of trying to scare off any bad-luck spirits that may be hovering about. And of course no birthday ever seems complete without the guests singing "Happy Birthday to You." This song was written around 1900 by two American women, Mildred J. Hill and Patty S. Hill. It has been a tradition ever since.

.   .   .

The games we play at birthday parties are often a symbol of trying to know the unknown. In this case, of course, the unknown is the future, or the new year of life that lies ahead for the birthday child.

One of the oldest birthday games is Pin the Tail on the Donkey. A large picture of a donkey without a tail is pinned to the wall. Each child at the party is given a donkey's tail made of paper and a pin to stick through it. Then, one by one, the children are blindfolded. They are spun around a few times and pointed in the direction of the donkey. The child who pins the tail closest to where it should be on the donkey wins the prize.

There are other versions of this game, such as Pin the Nose on the Clown or Pin the Ear on the Bunny. But the idea of trying to guess correctly, while blindfolded, is the same.

Other blindfold games like Blind Man's Buff may be played at birthday parties. And "hiding games" like Hide and Seek, Tag, or Red Light are popular, too. Whoever is "it" must not see while the others scatter and hide. "It" has to catch one of the other players. Then that player becomes "it."

One of the most popular of all blindfold games played at birthday parties comes from Mexico and

other countries of Spanish-speaking America. It is known as Breaking the Piñata (pee-NYA-ta). A piñata can be bought in a store. Or it can be made at home from a cardboard box or from newspaper that is soaked in water and then molded and stiffened into a round or oval shape with a hollow center. The inside is then filled with candies and other goodies, and the opening is sealed. Small toys or party favors may also be put inside the piñata.

The outside of the piñata may be covered with frilly colored paper and trimmed with fringe or paper streamers. It may look like a clown, a puppet, a bird, a monkey, or some other animal or object. The piñata is hung overhead in a playroom, garage, garden, or other large space. It can usually be raised or lowered by a rope.

Each child at the party is blindfolded in turn and given a long stick to poke the piñata and try to break it. At first the children's sticks may only make a small hole or crack in the piñata. But sooner or later the piñata will break, and all its goodies will come tumbling down for the party-goers to share. The blindfolded players have really been hunting in the dark for a sign of good luck for the coming year.

A Treasure Hunt is another game in which the players must search the unknown. Sometimes it is played by the birthday child, who is hunting for hidden presents. Sometimes there are hidden presents for all the party guests to find.

The Treasure Hunt begins with a written clue that might be in the form of a rhyme. For example:

Walk straight ahead
And follow your feet
To a box in the kitchen
With something to eat.

The "box" might be the refrigerator, a breadbox, a cereal box, or some other kind of box. Inside the correct box will be another clue. It may lead to someplace else in the house, such as under a bed, inside a closet, or behind a sofa cushion. Each clue will lead to the next until the present or presents that are the "treasure" are found.

A Scavenger Hunt is a little different. A time limit is set for finding a list of items. Some examples would be a bottle cap, a paper clip, a button, a shoelace, a penny with a certain year on it, a drinking straw, a Popsicle stick. Usually the places to scavenge are limited, too. The person who brings in the most items on the list wins a prize.

Of course almost any game, from Musical Chairs to Charades, may be played at birthday parties. The winners of the various party games usually take home prizes. But some party-givers see to it that everybody takes home a small gift as a memento. The Egyptian pharaohs were said to have given rich presents of gold and precious stones to their party guests.

At children's parties there may be a grab bag for the guests. The little packages might contain candies, a Yo-Yo, a set of crayons or felt-tip pens, a comic book, a bubble-making ring, or other small toys or games.

The gifts that everyone is most excited about, though, are the ones that have been brought to the birthday child. These presents are usually opened at the party so everyone can admire them. They, too, are a form of well-wishing.

Finally the last guest leaves, the party is over, and the new year of life is about to begin in earnest. It is hoped that all the birthday rituals and ceremonies will have worked their magic and that the year ahead will indeed be a happy one.

5

Which Birthdays Are Special?

A birthday is always a very special day. So it's hard to say that any one birthday is more important than any other. Yet, in various parts of the world, certain birthdays are treated as special events because a key point in life has been reached. These points are sometimes known as milestones.

Birth itself is, of course, a time of celebration. Many peoples have special ceremonies to welcome the newborn. In Egypt, for example, a party is given for the one-week-old infant. This custom is also observed in some other countries where most of the people are Moslems.

On the seventh day after birth, relatives, friends, neighbors, and children come to see the baby and wish it well. At the home of the newborn child there will be lighted candles, flowers, and samples of the fruits of the earth. Often each guest is given a small bag of dates, dried beans, cereal grains, nuts, and sweets. The child is also surrounded with these offerings, as well as bread and salt. Salt is sprinkled, too, over the heads of the guests. This part of the ceremony is usually carried out by the midwife who assisted in the birth of the child or by a grandmother or other older woman.

As Egypt is one of the world's oldest civilizations, its people have long known how important grains and other products of the soil are to life and growth. The same is true in other parts of the Middle East, for this is where farming first began. The ceremony of the one-week birthday closes with singing and dancing. It is one of the most important birthday celebrations in the child's life.

· · ·

In countries of the Far East, such as China, Japan, and Korea, the baby's one-year birthday is an important milestone, Although the Chinese consider that a child is already one year old at the time of birth, they believe the first year of life outside the mother's body to be the most dangerous. So parents and relatives are always happy to see that year completed in good health.

In most Far Eastern countries, red is the color of celebration. So eggs that have been dyed red are served at the one-year birthday feast. The egg itself is a symbol of life. Noodles, the longer the better, are another popular food on this occasion. They stand for longevity, or long life.

Often the family tries to see into the future at the baby's one-year birthday. It is a Far Eastern custom to place the child in the midst of many different objects, such as a book, a pen, a piece of cloth, an abacus (a counting frame), and so forth. Whichever object the child reaches for first tells what the child will grow up to be. Here are some of the forecasts:

book	—	scholar
pen	—	writer or poet
piece of cloth	—	tailor
abacus	—	merchant
coin	—	wealthy person
ruler	—	perfectionist

In many cases there will be no more birthday parties until another important milestone in life is reached. That could be the sixty-first birthday!

Many Far Eastern peoples believe that the years of old age last from forty to sixty. So age sixty-one is the beginning of a brand-new life and calls for a big birthday celebration.

This is a good time to check back to see if the fortune told sixty years earlier at one's first birthday party came true. Did the child who chose the pen grow up to become a famous poet? Did the child who chose the coin become very rich?

Among many Japanese families, there are other childhood birthdays that are considered special. It is believed that the most dangerous ages after the first year are three, five, and seven. So, in Japan, a festival is held each year on November 15 for girls of seven, boys of five, and all children of three. It is known as Shichi-Go-San, or Seven-Five-Three.

The children who have reached these birthdays in the past year are dressed in their best and taken by their parents to a religious shrine. Often the children wear beautiful kimonos tied with a wide sash. They carry paper bags that are decorated with good-luck signs.

The parents give thanks at the shrine and pray for continued health and good fortune for their children. Sometimes the priests give the children a few candies or other souvenirs of their visit to put in their paper bags.

Then the real fun begins. Near the shrine are stalls selling candies, good-luck tokens, and toys.

With their parents' permission, the children try to fill their bags before leaving the shrine.

Later, at home, there may even be a party and more presents to help celebrate the Seven-Five-Three festival.

. . .

In many parts of the world, of course, children do not celebrate their individual birth dates at all. Instead, traditional coming-of-age ceremonies are held. They are an important part of growing up. An entire age set, or age group, of boys or girls takes part in these ceremonies.

The purpose of the rituals is to teach the young people of the tribe or village the history, laws, beliefs, and customs of their people. Also, they must learn the songs and dances of the tribal ceremonies so that they, in turn, can pass them on to the next generation. Some African peoples consider that children as young as the nine to twelve age group are ready for initiation into the grown-up world.

Initiation usually means going through a number of tests. The young people may be sent away from their families to be instructed by elders or religious leaders of the tribe. They may be tested by having to remain silent for long periods. They may have to spend a great deal of time alone or lying very still in cramped quarters. Usually they will have to undergo the pain of being circumcised. And sometimes they will receive cuts on their faces, chests, or other parts of the body. The scars that result from these cuts are marks of belonging to the tribe. It is considered cowardly to cry out when the cuts are being made.

Masai boys aged thirteen to seventeen undergo a two-stage initiation. The Masai are a herding people of East Africa. They raise cattle and live mainly on the blood and the milk of their animals. The blood is drawn from the neck veins of living bulls.

The first stage of the Masai initiation lasts about three months. The boys leave their parents' homes, paint their bodies white, and are taught how to become young warriors. At the end of the first stage, the boys have their heads shaved. At this time, also, they are circumcised.

During the second stage, the young warriors grow their hair long. They live in a special camp, or warriors' village, called a *manyatta*, where they practice hunting the wild animals that might attack the Masai herds. The second stage usually lasts a few years. From that time on, the young Masai are full warriors. When they are ready, they will marry and become owners of large cattle herds like their fathers.

Masai girls are initiated into grown-up life when they are fourteen or fifteen. They, too, leave their homes and live in special huts. Older women teach them the duties of marriage and how to care for babies. Soon after that they marry and lead a life similar to that of their mothers.

• • •

An important milestone among Jews the world over is a boy's thirteenth birthday. This is the time of his entry into religious manhood. He becomes a *bar mitzvah*, or "son of the commandment." The celebration of this birthday is also called a Bar Mitzvah.

To prepare for his Bar Mitzvah, the boy may have spent years at study. He is expected to learn the Hebrew-language prayers, the laws, duties, and practices of his religion. The Bar Mitzvah ceremony itself is held in a synagogue on or near the day of his thirteenth birthday. Dressed in fine new clothes, the boy is called to the altar, where he recites a prayer or blessing and reads from the holy writings. Often, he also gives a

speech of thanks to his parents and teachers who are seated with the congregation.

Afterward there may be an offering of cake, wine, and other food for all who were present. Some Bar Mitzvah parties, following the service, are very lavish. Friends and relatives may be invited to a formal luncheon or evening party. The Bar Mitzvah boy receives presents. They are usually different from those he was given on earlier birthdays. Instead of toys, games, and novelties, he will receive books, writing materials, a briefcase, and other more grown-up items.

He may also be given a new Bible and a large silken prayer shawl. He now shares the religious responsibilities of his father and other grown men who observe the practices of Judaism. It is expected that he will say special morning prayers, attend synagogue services, and fast on Yom Kippur. That is the Hebrew holy day when adult Jews atone for their sins.

For girls of the Jewish faith, there can be a similar ceremony. It is known as Bas Mitzvah or Bat Mitzvah, and means "daughter of the commandment." This entry into womanhood usually takes place at age twelve or thirteen. According to ancient religious laws and customs, women do not

perform all of the rituals that men do. However, in some branches of modern Judaism, this is now changing. A number of women have even become rabbis in Reform congregations. Conservative congregations are also beginning to accept women as rabbis.

In many ways, the Jewish Bar Mitzvah and Bas Mitzvah are like the Confirmation ceremonies that take place in the various Christian churches. Among Christians there is a wider range of ages at which young people may be confirmed. But the basic idea is the same. They are making a pledge to take full part in their religion.

• • •

Growing up also means having more privileges as well as more duties. One of the most joyous birthday parties is the fifteenth *cumpleaños* (koom-play-AH-nyohs) for girls, as it is celebrated in Mexico, Puerto Rico, other parts of Spanish-speaking America, and Brazil. The Spanish word *cumpleaños* means "birthday," or "completed years."

Those families who can afford the expense are really giving their daughters a "coming-out" party. This event marks a girl's introduction to society. It announces that she is ready to start going out with young men and even to be courted for marriage.

On the morning of her fifteenth birthday, the girl and her family may go to Mass as they would on her saint's day, or name day. Afterward there may be a luncheon or open house for family members. But the real party begins in the evening.

If it is warm enough, the party may be held outdoors in a patio or garden. There will be colored lanterns, flowers, and a lavish buffet supper with fancy desserts. The young men arrive dressed in their best, and the hostess and other young women often wear long dresses. There will be music for dancing, and the party may go on into the early morning hours.

At a fifteenth birthday party in Mexico, a mariachi band of strolling musicians may also be present. Wearing dark, silver-studded costumes and large sombreros, the mariachis play guitars,

violins, and horns. They perform the traditional romantic music of Mexico. The name *mariachi* comes from the word "marriage." These musicians also play at weddings.

Once a girl has passed her fifteenth birthday, she may also be serenaded from time to time with an early-morning love song known as a *mañanita* (mah-nya-NEE-tah). It is played by hired mariachis. Usually the serenades are ordered for the morning of a young woman's name day or birthday by a young man who is trying to win her favor.

In the United States and Canada, the Sweet Sixteen party is similar to the fifteenth birthday celebration of Latin America. But in these North American countries, girls usually choose the kinds of parties they want. Some may prefer to give a luncheon, a skating-rink party, or even a slumber party for a small group of girls only. Others may invite boys as well to an informal party at home. Or there may be an elaborate celebration at a hotel or country club. At some parties the guests may arrive in jeans; at others they may be asked to wear formal clothes.

Sugar is the traditional symbol of the Sweet Sixteen party. Sometimes the hostess will wear a corsage of sugar cubes and satin ribbons. She may offer corsages to the other girls at the party, too. Some sixteen-year-olds, though, feel that these old-fashioned customs are too sentimental. Times have changed, they say. At sixteen, they are busy thinking about college and career choices. They may not want to have a Sweet Sixteen party at all.

Yet many girls still feel that a Sweet Sixteen party is important to them. It's one way of saying a fond farewell to the birthday parties of childhood. They think of it as being the last time they will have a chance to sit behind a big cake, make a wish, and blow out the candles before grown-up life begins in earnest.

* * *

In many parts of the world, of course, children are expected to take on grown-up duties at a very early age. Elsewhere, young people are considered grown-up when they are old enough to have a driver's license or old enough to vote. In Great Britain, being given the key to the house was once considered an important sign of adulthood. This used to take place at the age of twenty-one. It meant that a young man had his father's permission to come and go as he pleased and to stay out as late as he liked.

Nowadays, both young men and young women have more freedom at a much earlier age than twenty-one. Yet the "key-to-the-house" twenty-first birthday is still widely celebrated in England, Wales, Scotland, and Ireland, and also in Australia and New Zealand. It is still called a "coming of age."

The symbol of this milestone birthday is a large cardboard key covered with silvery paper. Often it is presented by the father of the twenty-one-year-old in front of all the party guests. The guests offer keys, too. Decorated silver-colored keys may come attached to twenty-first birthday cards. Or a tankard (a tall metal mug with a lid) that has a large key on it may be given as a gift.

Parents, relatives, and friends sometimes place announcements in the local newspapers offering their good wishes to the young man or woman who is just turning twenty-one. "Key-to-the-house" parties are always very jolly, and many toasts are made. The cake for this birthday is generally made up of two or three layers shaped like a wedding cake in a tower or pyramid form. The top is often decorated with a large "21." And no twenty-first birthday party is complete without the traditional birthday song that ends with the words:

> *Shout hip, hip, hooray,*
> *For I'm twenty-one today!*

Birth predictions, naming ceremonies, birthday parties, and coming-of-age celebrations are all part of the magic of having been born. Each family and each society has its own traditions and customs. Whatever form they take, the occasion is marked by hope. Good wishes are offered by all — for health, for growth, for self-fulfillment, and for many more happy days.

Index

Astrology, 13-17; horo-
scopes, 8, 14; zodiacs,
14-17

Baptisms, 31
Bible, 2, 60
Birth flowers, 10, 11-13
Birth records, 7
Birth signs, 14-16
Birthday beliefs, follow-
ing, 8-10
Birthday cakes, 8, 37,
38-39, 66
Birthday candles: blow-
ing out, 8; earliest use
of, 37-38; kinds of, 38
Birthday cards, 40
Birthday parties, 4, 19,
30, 40-48; beginning
of, 37-38; games at,
42-46; prizes and gifts
for guests, 46-48;

special, 51-56, 59,
62-63, 64-66
Birthday presents, 48
Birthday rhyme, telling
the future by, 9-10
Birthday serenades, 63
Birthday smacks, spanks,
bumps, etc., 40-42
Birthdays: early celebra-
tions, 2; how remem-
bered in prehistoric
times, 1-2; of im-
portant people, 4;
personal, 4-5, 19
Birthstones, 8, 10-13
Blindfold games, 42-45
Breaking the Piñata, 45

Caesar, Julius, 2-3
Calendars: age of, 17;
before, 1-2; begin-

nings of, 2; Gregorian, 3; Julian, 3

Candles, origin of, 37

Celebrations: birthday, 4, 19, 30, 37-38, 40-48; Chinese New Year, 17-18; christenings and baptisms, 31; Christmas, 4; name-day, 28-29, 30; special birthdays, 51-66

Chinese calendar, 17

Chinese New Year, 4, 17-18; as giant birth-day party, 18

Chinese zodiac, 16-17

Christ, Jesus, 4, 29-30

Christenings, 31

Christmas, 4

Coming-of-age cere-monies, 56-61; Con-firmation, 61; Jewish, 59-61; Masai, 57-59

Cumpleaños, Hispanic, 62-63

Future, telling the, 7-10; by astrology, 13-17; by baby's choice of objects, 52-53; with party games, 42-46

Games, party, 42-46

Godparents, role of, 32-33

"Happy Birthday to You," 42

Hidden objects inside birthday cakes, 39

Hill, Mildred J. and Patty S., 42

Horoscopes, 8, 14

Islam, 4

Jewish coming-of-age ceremonies, 59-61; Bar Mitzvah, 59-60; Bas (Bat) Mitzvah, 61

Key-to-the-house parties, 65-66

Mariachi bands, 62-63

Masai coming-of-age ceremonies, 57-59; boys, 57-58; girls, 58-59

Milestones. *See* Special birthdays

Mohammed, Prophet, 4

Name-day celebrations, 28-29, 30

Names, 21-30; after the Holy Family, 29-30; being comfortable with, 33-35; changing, 35; choosing, 27-30; from dead relatives,

27-28; new and old, 22;
from saints, 28-29, 30;
significance of, 22-27
Naming the baby, 31-32;
christening or bap-
tism, 31; by godfather,
32; hiding the name,
31-32
Noisemakers to scare off
bad-luck spirits, 42

Parties. *See* Birthday
parties; Celebrations
Pin the Tail on the
Donkey, 42
Piñatas, 45
Predictions and proph-
ecies at birth, 7-8

Sabbath day, 9, 10
Saints' days, 4
Scavenger Hunts, 46
Seventh-Day Advent-
ists, 10
Shichi-Go-San festival,
55-56
Silver spoons, 32-33
Special birthdays, 51-66;

coming-of-age cere-
monies, 56-61; Far
East one-year, 52-53;
Hispanic *cumpleaños*,
62-63; Japanese Shichi-
Go-San, 55-56; key-
to-the-house parties,
65-66; Middle East
one-week, 51-52;
sixty-first, 53-54;
Sweet Sixteen parties,
64-65; twenty-first,
65-66
Stories and legends of
births, 7
Sweet Sixteen parties,
64-65

Treasure Hunts, 45-46
Tree-planting for birth
of child, 13

Wishes, birthday, 38

Yom Kippur, 60

Zodiac, 14-16; Chinese,
16-17; signs (symbols)
of, 14-16